We Make an App

Careers in Computers

Sonja Reyes

COMPUTER SCIENCE For the REAL World™

Rosen Classroom™

Published in 2018 by The Rosen Publishing Group, Inc.
29 East 21st Street, New York, NY 10010

Book Design: Jennifer Ryder-Talbot
Editor: Caitie McAneney

All illustrations by Contentra Technologies

Library of Congress Cataloging-in-Publication Data

Names: Reyes, Sonja.
Title: We make an app: careers in computers / Sonja Reyes.
Description: New York : Rosen Classroom, 2018. | Series: Computer Kids: Powered by Computational Thinking | Includes glossary and index.
Identifiers: LCCN ISBN 9781508137740 (pbk.) | ISBN 9781538324400 (library bound) | ISBN 9781538355411 (6pack) | ISBN 9781538352755 (ebook)
Subjects: LCSH: Application software--Juvenile fiction.
Classification: LCC PZ7.R494 We 2018 | DDC [E]--dc23

Manufactured in the United States of America

CPSIA Compliance Information: Batch #WS18RC: For Further Information contact Rosen Publishing, New York, New York at 1-800-237-9932

Table of Contents

What's an App? **5**

A Possible Career **6**

Brainstorming **8**

A Problem to Solve **11**

Setting It Apart **12**

How Will It Look? **14**

Building the App **17**

Our User Interface **18**

Testing **21**

Releasing Our App **22**

Glossary **23**

Index **24**

What's an App?

I got a phone for my birthday! It's a smartphone, which means I can access the Internet on it. I play around with my phone to learn about its **functions**.

There are small images on the main screen. My brother says these are called apps. If I tap on an image, then it opens an app. "What's an app?" I ask. My brother says "app" is short for "application." It's like a computer program that does a certain thing. I can download new apps, too. There are apps for health and fitness, learning new languages, and taking pictures.

A Possible Career

My brother says that people can make a career out of creating apps. If someone knows how to code, then making an app is easy. Some programs online can help people make an app even if they aren't **experts** at coding.

People can sell apps to make money. They do this by charging money to download the app. Other people get money from companies that put advertisements on the app. In order to sell an app, the app must fill a need. It must be something that people will find fun, useful, or necessary to everyday life.

Brainstorming

I have friends who are great at coding. We learn about coding in our computer science class. I ask my friends if they want to make an app together. They think it's a great idea!

First, we brainstorm an idea for an app. We have many ideas. What will it do? What will it look like? What problem will it solve? We want our app to be educational and fun. We also want it to be colorful and **interactive**. That means users press buttons to give input, and then they get a response from the app.

A Problem to Solve

"What problem will our app solve?" I ask my friends. That's the big question. The rest of the app will be created as a solution to this problem.

"We have a social studies test coming up," my friend Lily says. "Maybe we could create an app that will help people study for the big exam." I think that's a great idea! Our app could have **visuals** of social studies facts and information. It could also have an interactive quiz. Users could take the quiz to see what they know about social studies topics, and what they should work on.

Setting It Apart

We want our app to be useful to students not only at our school, but all over the world. We want to cover social studies topics such as history, **economics**, geography, and civics. Civics is the study of being a good citizen.

Our app needs to be set apart from other educational apps that exist. We research other apps. We get some great ideas about **graphics** and quiz formats. We come up with ideas about how our app will be different. We will call it "Super Social Studies Kids!" It will have fun cartoons and a flashcard feature for studying.

How Will It Look?

We sketch ideas about how we want our app to look. I draw images of what the screen would look like. My friends and I come up with text, quiz questions, and graphics that we want to include in our app.

Now, it's time to create a wireframe, or basic model, of the app. We use an online tool to help us create the wireframe. We input our text and graphics into the online tool, and then we can see what our app would look like. We decide which buttons the user would be able to press and where each button would take the user.

Building the App

We create a storyboard for our app. The storyboard is like a map through the app. It helps us **visualize** what will happen on each screen and how to **navigate** the app. Creating the wireframe and storyboard take the longest amount of time. We want to make sure to get everything just right.

It's important to be very clear about every single part of the app. We have to make **detailed** diagrams to show what each step will look like. We have to think about the functions users will be interacting with, but also the "backend" applications they won't see.

Our User Interface

Our computer science teacher helps us build our user interface, or UI. The user interface is what the user sees when they interact with the app. People like apps that are designed well. Good apps often have a clean, fun design that is easy to navigate.

We show our teacher our wireframe and get her feedback about our design. She gives us some advice. For example, she says we should keep it simple with the design and not add too many crazy graphics. Our teacher **introduces** us to a real graphic designer who will help us make our sketches into reality.

Testing

We use an online app-building tool to help us bring our ideas to life. However, there's one more important step we need to take before releasing our app.

It's important to test any computer program before releasing it. Real computer programmers check their work again and again to make sure there are no bugs, or mistakes, in it. Through all of our work, we've built a **prototype**. We make sure all of the buttons work. We take our quizzes to make sure the correct answers are recorded. There are a few bugs the first time we try it out, but we find them and fix them.

Releasing Our App

Our app has been designed, built, and tested. Now it's time to release it into the world! How can we do that? We research different online stores that sell apps, such as the Google Play store. Once we release our app, people will be able to use it. We hope they can learn something about social studies from our app!

Building apps isn't just a fun project or hobby. Some people build apps as a source of **income**. App development has become an exciting career. If you have a great idea, you can build an app, too!

Glossary

detail: Attention to the small parts of something.

economics: A social science concerned with the creating, selling, and buying of goods and services.

expert: Someone with great knowledge about a certain subject.

function: The action for which a person or thing is specially fitted or used for.

graphic: A picture that represents or illustrates something.

income: The money that one makes from doing a job or selling something.

interactive: Having to do with the actions of a user.

introduce: To cause people to meet.

navigate: To find one's way.

prototype: An early model on which later models are based.

visual: Something, such as a graphic, that is used for effect or illustration.

visualize: To picture something.

Index

B

bugs, 21

C

civics, 12

code, 6, 8

D

detail, 17

diagram, 17

E

economics, 12

educational, 9, 12

expert, 6

F

function, 5, 17

G

Google Play, 22

graphic, 12, 14, 15, 19

I

income, 22

interactive, 9, 11

introduce, 19

N

navigate, 17, 18

P

prototype, 21

S

storyboard, 17

V

visual, 11

visualize, 17

W

wireframe, 14, 15, 17, 19